UNSINKABLE

HOW TO BUILD PLYWOOD PONTOONS & LONGtAiL BOAt MOtORS out OF SCRAP

RoBNoxiouS

THERE'S A HISTORY OF PUNKS, AND OTHERLY IDENTIFIED PEOPLE, BUILDING SHANTY BOATS AND GOING DOWN RIVERS IN THE MISSISSIPPI BASIN.

Someone gets an idea in their head and outlines it to a receptive friend. Perhaps while sitting around a camp fire talking about journeys in years past, someone says, "Hey, let's build a shanty boat and float it down the Missouri River, move on to a different river, explore the whole basin of the Midwest! Everything would be made of scrap, even the boat motors." Peat and I talked about building a boat together. He convinced our friends Fern and Bella to join us and help build it. Plus, Ged the dog would be coming! Zoe and Savannah decided to throw a sleek aluminum john boat rig together and go boating, bringing Willard the dog! Two or more boats, each with a dog aboard, equals a boat punk flotilla.

We started with an easy project, making steel Danforth anchors. We used Gerty's shop in Minneapolis for the measuring, chopping, grinding, and welding! Zoe and I each made an anchor using the Gertrude/Danforth design.

I had already made a pair of sexy cedar paddles in Peat and Gerty's wood shop, located in the old Spice Factory, to propel my 17-foot-long Herters Wilderness Canoe. We brought the canoe for expeditions away from the big shanty boat.

The collecting began: metal, wood, foam, buckets, life jackets, engines, rope, chain, tarps, tents, rubber boots, rain coats, sparkling hotpants, money, tools, a sewing kit, a camera, binoculars, matches, lighters, river charts, steel cooking grill, pots, pans, food, and a typewriter with paper. This was gonna be awesome!

The local DIY venue, "Mala Zimmetbaum's Studio for Fine Arts & the Advancement of Wayward Youth," closed down. We went there and scored a bunch of pink foam from the walls: foam floats! We obtained five-gallon buckets and empty grease jugs from behind restaurants and grocery stores. We found other random foam chunks used for packing electronics that we planned to stuff the pontoons with. Old metal bed frames for the longtail motors were easily found scattered through the alleys of Minneapolis during spring-cleaning season. River charts were printed at the library from www.nwk.usace.army.mil/RiverCharts. Life jackets, raincoats, tents, cooking items, and so much more came from the thrift stores.

As the snow melted and the weather got warm, we starting building pontoons and boat motors. Our plan was to get as much done in Minneapolis as we could, then load it all on Peat's van and drive to The Crooked Hat, our friend's house in Kansas City, to finish and launch the boat on the Missouri River. After that, we planned to float as far down as we could; all the way to the Gulf; to the edges of madness and death.

Peat and Fern relax onboard *THE SNOWBALL* during the golden hour.

Fern and Bella on *THE SNOWBALL*.

Building a Longtail Boat Motor from Scrap

PEAT AND I DECIDED TO BUILD LONGTAIL BOAT MOTORS AT GERTY'S SHOP. *Having two motors would be better. If one broke down, we could run on the other one.*

I got a 3.5hp Briggs & Stratton engine from a guy on Craigslist; 50 bucks, never used. Peat used a 5hp engine which we mostly ended up using because our boat was big. The propeller was $20 from Youngs (youngprops.com), the U-joint $8 at a scrap store called Ambles, the axle was $10 at a hardware store. All the rest was scrap metal: steel bedframes found in alleys, pipes in abandoned buildings. Total cost, adding welding supplies and hardware, would be about a hundred bucks. The big cost is time. You also have to hope you did it right and it works. Having a friend with a welder and metal shop was very helpful.

Peat recently built a fancy longtail engine and used sealed bearings between the outer shaft and the solid inner drive shaft. This seems like a good idea, because at the end of our journey, the outer shafts of our motors were worn through by the action of the spinning inner shaft. Having the drive shaft run on sealed bearings must increase the fuel efficiency too, offering less resistance.

The U-joint connects the horizontal shaft of the engine to the drive shaft. A hard steel round stock is used for the drive shaft. This is slid inside an outer shaft which is U-bolted to the L stock which extends out some seven feet. A T-15 die-cast aluminum trolling motor propeller from Young Props (youngprops.com) is tapped and died onto the end of the drive shaft. These props are normally used to replace the worn out props on old trolling motors but they seem to work well on our longtail engines. Normal props used on boat motors in south-east Asia don't seem to work well on United States motors because the RPMs of U.S. are much higher than those sold in south-east Asia.

The fuel efficiency of the 5hp longtail motors was very good compared to normal boat motors: 30 miles to the gallon or more. We always ran the engine at about half throttle to extend the life of the engine and save on fuel. Most folks on the water are weekend warriors and not content to go at a speed that is hardly faster than walking. So, instead of our 5hp motor they would run a big gas-guzzling beast of a motor, then on Monday go back to work to pay for all the gas! Unlike a road trip in a car, we could turn off the motor and coast for miles. When the current was good, and the current was often very good on the Missouri River because there are no locks or dams, we could turn off the engine and drift in peace, listening to the birds and the wind.

I welded hinges onto my longtail frame and lag-bolted it to the transom of the boat so the drive shaft could be raised or lowered into the water. Steering would happen with the use of a rudder placed in the center. In south-east Asia, longtails are set on a pivot mount so the engine can be moved up and down and side to side, which is how the boat is steered. We decided it would be easier to just drop the motor in the water in a fixed position and steer using an easier-to-maneuver rudder.

A word of advice that we never follow: test the motor out before going on an epic adventure!

THE LONGTAIL BOAT MOTOR

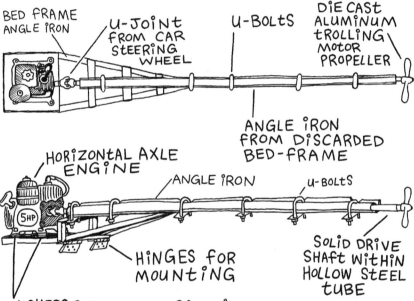

BED FRAME ANGLE IRON

U-JOINT FROM CAR STEERING WHEEL

U-BOLTS

DIE CAST ALUMINUM tROLLING MOTOR PROPELLER

ANGLE IRON FROM DISCARDED BED-FRAME

HORIZONTAL AXLE ENGINE

ANGLE IRON

U-BOLTS

5HP

HINGES FOR MOUNTING

SOLID DRIVE SHAFT WITHIN HOLLOW STEEL TUBE

WASHERS BETWEEN ENGINE & MOUNTING PLATE TO PRECISELY LEVEL WITH THE DRIVE SHAFT

TOOLS: METAL CHOP-SAW, WELDING MACHINE, METAL GRINDER, CLAMPS, METAL DRILL BITS, DRILL, RATCHET WRENCH SOCKET SET, THREAD LOCK COMPOUND FOR PROP, THREAD TAP & DIE SET.

The U-Joint connecting the drive shaft to the engine.

Two longtail motors, rudder in the center.

As often as possible, turn off the motor and drift! Ahhh... Yeah.

PLYWOOD PONTOONS

BOXED OUT ON ALL EDGES &
JOINTS WITH PINE 2×4s

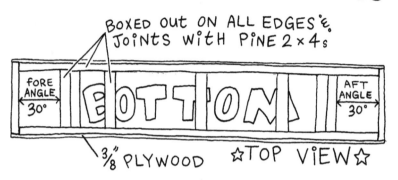

FORE ANGLE 30°

BOTTOM

AFT ANGLE 30°

3/8" PLYWOOD   ☆TOP VIEW☆

☆SIDE VIEW OF 2×4 STRUCTURE☆

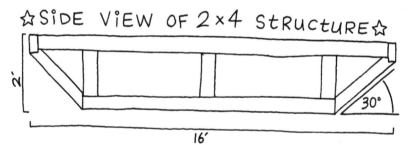

2'

30°

16'

FILL PONTOONS WITH STYROFOAM, PLASTIC
BOTTLES, 5 GALLON BUCKETS, ANYTHING THAT
HOLDS AIR! SEAL TOP OF PONTOON WITH PLYWOOD.
THE PONTOONS ARE NOW UN-SINKABLE.

SHEET FOAM

PACKING PEANUTS

PLASTIC BOTTLES
COLA

5 GALLON BUCKET

5 GALLON OIL JUGS

Building Plywood Pontoons From Scrap

WE USED SALVAGED 1/4" AND 3/8" PLYWOOD
FOR THE OUTSIDE AND 2x4S FOR THE FRAMING. *The wood came mostly from construction dumpsters. Some of it was hauled on my no-weld bicycle flatbed trailer, which could haul 4'x8' sheets of plywood and cause an instant parade on any street.*

The final dimensions of our pontoons were 20' long, 2' wide, 2' deep. Actually, I think they were a bit thinner or shorter, but 2'x2' is the dimension we wished we would have made them, so I won't post the actual undersized measurements. With five in the crew, *The Snowball* drafts halfway up the side on the pontoon. Not bad. The front of the pontoon had a good hydro-dynamic angle to it, 30 degrees. We should have done the same angle in the rear too, giving the pontoons that hydro-dynamically desirable "duck-like" body. With less resistance in the water you get better "Miles Per Gallon"!

We built our pontoons in three separate sections that would be easier to transport to Kansas City in the van: two 8' sections and one 4' section per pontoon. Arriving in KCMO, we glued and bolted the pontoon sections together. This worked, but also created weak spots where the sections joined together.

To make the framework for the pontoon, we cut the 2x4s and then held them together with pipe clamps to make the screwing-together easier. After the 2x4 frame was done, we cut the plywood to fit and screwed it on. We had to buy the wood screws and glue (Tightbond III with the duck on it), these things we could not salvage or dumpster.

After completing the pontoons, we needed to fill them with floaty stuff: foam, buckets, plastic bottles. This also came from construction dumpsters, alleyways, and from behind electronic stores, where there is always a lot of styrofoam, and from the dumpster area of restaurants. Peat was of the opinion that the pink or blue sheet foam was the best. I took a hammer and knocked down the lids of the five-gallon buckets, to make sure they were sealed. I double-checked the five-gallon grease jug lids to make sure the lids were on hellatight. Once we had stuffed every last hole in the pontoons with floating stuff, we put the 1/2" plywood tops onto the pontoons and screwed them down: river-ready pontoons.

At our beach launching point the two pontoons were then wrangled down to the river with the help of a few friends and then connected with 2x4"s bolted into the pontoons with lag bolts. We used 8' long 2x4s, so the final boat dimensions were 8' wide by 20' long. It's a minimal space for four people and one large dog to attempt an extended voyage!

The last thing to go on was the thicker 3/4" decking plywood. The pontoons were now a boat! We attached the two longtail engines, the rudder, and screwed down four benches onto the outside of the deck. Yet to come was some kind of roof structure from woody material that we would find along the river, being hopeful that rain wasn't forecast in the near future.

We spent less than $100 on the pontoon boat itself. So much of the material was free for the taking that we saved our cash to spend in the strange and sweet towns along the river.

Foam and five-gallon buckets stuffed in pontoon.

Fern, Bella, and Peat stuff the pontoons with foam, buckets, and jugs.

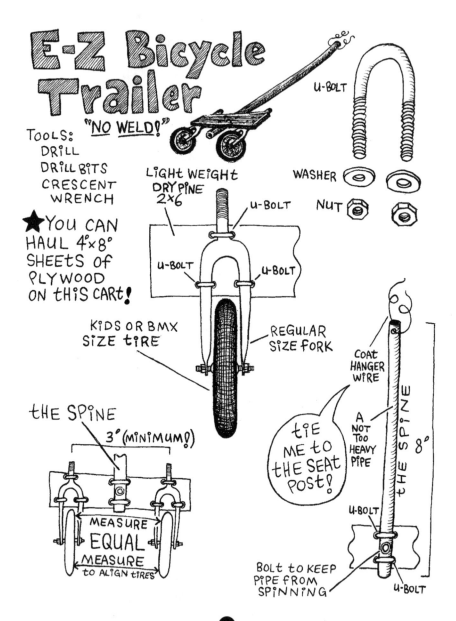

E-Z Bicycle Trailer

"NO WELD!"

TOOLS:
DRILL
DRILL BITS
CRESCENT
WRENCH

★ YOU CAN HAUL 4'x8' SHEETS OF PLYWOOD ON THIS CART!

U-BOLT

WASHER

NUT

LIGHT WEIGHT DRY PINE 2x6

U-BOLT

U-BOLT   U-BOLT

KIDS OR BMX SIZE TIRE

REGULAR SIZE FORK

THE SPINE

3' (MINIMUM!)

MEASURE
EQUAL
MEASURE
to ALIGN TIRES

TIE ME to THE SEAT POST!

COAT HANGER WIRE

A NOT TOO HEAVY PIPE

THE SPINE 8'

U-BOLT

BOLT TO KEEP PIPE FROM SPINNING

U-BOLT

The E-Z Bicycle Flatbed Trailer
The bicycle flatbed was very useful for
cruising the productive alleyways of Minneapolis for springtime project scraps: sheets of foam, plywood, 2x4"s, metal bed frames, and other golden opportunities for shanty boat building.

My trailer was built with an 8' long steel pipe for the main spine, this came from an old cyclone fence, the sort you might find surrounding the dog dropping covered grass of many a city home. This pipe was then attached to a 4' wide piece of lightweight pine 2x6 using U-Bolts and a bolt drilled thru the center to keep the spine from sliding and spinning.

Next I found two similar bicycle forks from a normal size bicycle. These I attached with the same method as the center pole to each side of the 4' wide plank. I obtained two similar sized child bicycle tires and mounted these in normal size forks with the same axle length! The extra space in the forks is used to mount them so that they do not spin. The two sides of the fork rest solidly upon the wood and prevent it from spinning. One does not even need to steal these tires from children who have foolishly left their bikes on the sidewalk, the tires can be found in trash piles in the alley ways; last year's toy abused, broken and discarded, but inevitably with a perfectly good front tire. One child's junk is another person's toy.

The final touch was the easiest: a hole was drilled through the far end of the 8' long pole and a length of coat hanger wire was fed through, the most simple hitch! All one had to do then was tie the wire to the seat post or to the rear cargo rack, creating a rudimentary U-joint. One could also arrange a fancier and better balanced hitch attached to the bike frame back by the rear axle. This would be preferable, as then the weight of the cart would not be pushing the bicycle over. For simplicity and expedience, there is nothing quite like a piece of coat hanger to hold it all together.

Mount some red reflectors on the rear of your flatbed bicycle trailer, some yellow ones on the sides. Now, take the streets! Take a full lane! You can even take your time.

The E-Z bicycle flatbed trailer. Able to haul 4x8 sheets of plywood! Attach a bucket seat with seat belt to the cart and haul your drunk friends around!

WITH THE HELP OF A FEW FRIENDS WE HAVE FLOATING PONTOON BOAT. THANKS, FRIENDS.

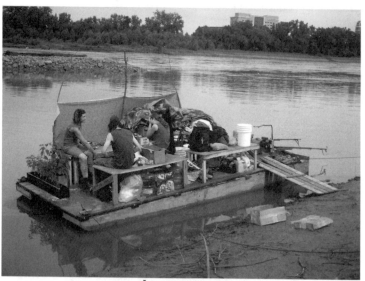

LOOKS READY TO GO.

THE FLIGHT OF THE SNOWBALL

KANSAS CITY TO CARUTHERSVILLE. PEAT, FERN, BELLA, GED THE DOG, AND I ARRIVED IN KANSAS CITY, MO AND GOT RIGHT TO WORK AT THE CROOKED HAT HOUSE ASSEMBLING THE PONTOONS.

We sawed and we screwed. We ate, drank, and had fun! We called our boat *The Snowball* because it would pick up stuff while going downhill. The crew of our sister boat, *The Two Headed Dog*, had been in town a long time and couldn't stand loitering about any longer. We drove them down to the boat ramp. The launch of *The Two Headed Dog* was smooth like chunky peanut butter. Moments after the boat was floating, Willard jumped out and swam back to shore. They had to come back in and get him. Eventually, he stopped jumping off the boat.

Many days later it was our turn. We stood at the River Front Recreation Park at Mile 363 of the Missouri River, 363 miles upriver from the confluence of the Mississippi River where the measurement of the Missouri River begins at Mile 0. With the help of a few friends we slid each pontoon down the bank to the beach and then into the water. It's always good to see that a boat you made actually floats. Yeehaw! We attached the pontoons to each other with 2x6s and then sheeted the top with plywood. On top of that went four benches to be nailed down on the deck. On top of the van, my canoe, THE SAUCER, was brought down to be tied alongside. We had no roof as yet, but the forecast was good for days.

One day, the water patrol stopped by in a patrol boat and checked our paperwork. We had registered the pontoon boat in Minnesota where it is a simple thing to register a home-made boat, you don't even have to show it to them, only describe it and pay the price-per-foot. We told the water patrolman we were going all the way to the Gulf. He shook my hand enthusiastically, then went to go catch the Blue Angels air show. He could have hung out with us drinking light beer, as the Blue Angels flew right over the river as we continued with minor adjustments on our own screaming machine.

Having received our fly-over, it was now officially time to go boating!

WAVERLY

GLASGOW

☆ KCMO

Our journey
began here...

MISSISSIPPI RIVER

MISSOURI RIVER

JEFFERSON CITY

CHAMOIS

HERMANN

St. CHARLES

thE 2 HEADED
DOG SINKS

● St. Louis

the flight
of the
Snowball
☆ in the year 2008 ☆

SAINT
GENEVIEVE ●

● GRAND
TOWER

CAPE
GIRARDEAU ●

OHIO RIVER

● CAIRO
(KAY-RO)

NEW
MADRID

☆ CARUTHERSVILLE

...our journey
ended here.

LOWER MISSISSIPPI R.

TIPTONVILLE

● MEMPHIS

"SEAN GREEN TEETH PLAYED US A LITTLE TUNE ON HIS CLARINET AND GAVE US A DIRTY PLAYING CARD WITH A LADY ON IT WHICH FERN AND I MADE A TIN CAN BEJEWELED SHRINE FOR." —Bella

RENDEZVOUS WITH THE TWO HEADED DOG.
MILE 335.7, SIBLEY BEND. WE MADE 28 MILES ON OUR FIRST DAY. A PART OF OUR SUPPER THAT NIGHT WAS WOOD NETTLE AND STINGING NETTLE THAT I FOUND UNDER A TREE CANOPY. *Our camp was a half-mile downriver from a sand bar with several aluminum john boats and yahoos shooting guns. The sun was setting and we didn't have lights to boat at night. Is this far enough away from them, we wondered?* No, it wasn't. All night long they were blazing around with spotlights and shotguns. Hunting? I am unfamiliar with this style. This seemed like the behavior of tweakers. In the morning, they roared up to our camp and asked if we had any weed for sale.

The next day, 16 miles down the river at Bootlegger Bend, we spied a slow moving vessel ahead on the shimmering water. Could it be *The Two Headed Dog*? The structure was hard to mistake, nobody else had janky tarp roofs on their boats! We drew near, close enough to see their gleaming white teeth smiling at us, and then Willard the dog jumped into the water and swam for *The Snowball*! Willard and Ged had a dog reunion. Truly, now we were boating. The flotilla was united!

That evening we camped at Mile 317, finding wild grapes growing on shore. Savannah and I canoed and then walked into Lexington to get some cold ones, then got a ride back to the river in the bed of a pick-up truck with a fisherman and his wife. The fisherman bragged about how his wife was so buff she could carry the outboard motor.

INVASIVE ASIAN FLYING CARP!

BY SAVANNAH

BY THE FALL OF 2011, ALMOST ANYONE WHO LIVES ALONG THE MISSISSIPPI MUST HAVE HEARD THE HORROR STORIES ABOUT "INVASIVE FLYING ASIAN CARP." *We read newspaper articles about how the fish are moving upriver, and how the city of Chicago has put a giant net into Lake Michigan to try to stop them.* We have heard questions as to whether the fish are really Asian, or even carp at all. We have heard, many times over, the prediction that nets and dams will do nothing to stop them: It's only a matter of time before the Flying Asian Carp reach all the way up to Lake Itasca, and that pleasure boating will never be the same.

At the time, neither Zoe nor I had ever heard of this phenomenon. The idea of giant fish flinging themselves out of the water directly at our heads would have sounded to us like only one of my many unlikely, bizarrely unfounded anxieties about boating in strange new waters.

I had been boating only once before, for one month down the Ohio, as a guest on Zoe and Paula's boat THE MAUDREY-JEAN. For that month I was referred to as the "hobble-de-hoy." I let Zoe and Paula study the charts, start the motor, jump in the water to tow the boat through sand-bars, throw in the anchor, and change the spark-plugs while I sat in the shade and drank beer. My job was to look out for buoys. Zoe and Paula were very involved in trying to learn everything there was to know about boating, but my main interest was keeping up my constant, vigilant hunt for fish. Living or dead.

I was proud that I had the courage to go boating at all.

I have what I usually describe as a "thing about fish." It's a constant awareness, not fear as much as an intense alertness to the possibility of fish. I am not afraid of fish; I am afraid of being surprised by fish. Before this boat trip I had two main concerns:

1) Fish flying through the air without warning.

2) Being forced, for some reason, to bite down on the tail of a living, still wet and flapping fish. I often get hung up on the sound: the small crunch that I imagine this act would produce.

I am constantly looking for fish. When walking down a city sidewalk, if I see a piece of garbage, my first thought is, "A fish? No, it's a piece of garbage." Every rock in the water is a potential fish. A sponge in the bathroom, a tin can in the alley, a shoe half hidden under my bed: all potential fish.

Frequently Asked Questions:
Q: Did you have a traumatic childhood experience with a fish?
A: No. Not that I remember.
Q: They're not going to bite you.
A: I am aware of that. It's not about them biting me.
Q: You're just afraid that they are going to unexpectedly fly through the air? A: Yes.
Q: That doesn't seem very likely.
A: It doesn't.
Q: But you are still afraid of it.
A: I am alert to the possibility.

I decided to push through my fears and go boating with Zoe all summer long, from Kansas City down to New Orleans. Our boat, *The Two Headed Dog*, was a day or two ahead of our friends on *The Snowball*. Zoe and I were in the water floating slowly downstream and exploring some little creeks and tributaries while we waited for them to catch up to us.

As we floated down, we saw a creek that the river flowed into, and after consulting our charts thought that it might be a loop that would bring us back into the main body of the Missouri a few miles downstream. It was a beautiful, shady creek filled with tiny fish just visible in the clear water. Zoe was rowing with our homemade wooden oars. I was dragging my hand in the water and resting my feet on the dog's back. He had been asleep all morning. We had a little battery-run tape player and were listening to the Shirelles.

After about 20 minutes the creek started getting shallower and shallower and, eventually, we couldn't get through. We turned around to head back, and now, against the current, we pulled in the oars and started up the motor. I was just learning how to motor and I volunteered to steer us back. After a few false starts I got it going and sat in the back with the motor behind me, facing front. Willard took up most of the middle and Zoe was in the front seat, leaning back and facing me.

The Two Headed Dog was covered with a kind of metal cage—a thick wire grid that created a long rounded shape like a covered wagon. We had intended to use a few pieces of PVC pipe to hold up our tarp like most of the other boats, but we happened to find this piece of metal wiring in an alleyway in Kansas City, and it was easy enough to bend it into a half circle and bolt it to the sides of the hull. It carried our tarp rolled up on top, and we hung pots and pans and lanterns and drying laundry from the inside of it. We had no idea when we put it on, but it was also the only barrier between us and the attack-fish of the lower Missouri.

As I was motoring I heard a kind of "ka-thunk!" behind me and felt the motor jump. "What was that?" I asked Zoe. "Is that normal?"

"Can I motor for a minute?" she asked me in a very calm voice.

We switched places and I sat down facing her. "Don't freak out," she said, "but that was a fish. A big fish just jumped out and hit the motor."

"No, seriously. What was it?"

Ka-THUNK! I saw it this time—a huge flattish fish, probably 15-inches-long, jumped out of the water and bounced off the cage right by my head.

We both started screaming. Zoe motored faster, but the faster we went the quicker the fish came at us. In a minute, they were as thick as popcorn, one after another, bouncing off of the cage and splashing back into the water. I don't know what we looked or sounded like, but Zoe remembers us both screaming repetitive, obscene gibberish. I was probably crying. I went up to defend the open front of the cage. I crouched near the opening, holding a piece of a broken oar like a baseball bat, prepared to smack a fish out of our home. If a fish had gotten past me, the cage that was keeping most of them out would probably have kept it bouncing around inside the boat. Thank God, Zoe was motoring as fast as she could. They just continued loudly bouncing off the sides. These were big fish. Between the propellers and the fish splashing in and out, the water was churned up all around us like it was boiling.

I have no idea how long this went on, but after awhile they suddenly stopped. It didn't taper off—it went from 30 fish per minute to zero. We looked behind us and saw them all still jumping out of the water, but only up to a specific line, like an invisible barrier was holding them back.

We caught our breath as we motored back into the main current of the river. We noticed that the tape of the Shirelles was still playing, and that the dog was still asleep.

When we calmed down, we found a fishing boat and pulled up to ask what the hell just happened. The fishermen were sympathetic—they told us that some people had begun wearing football helmets while boating, because the bigger specimens of Flying Carp were known to leap out of the water and hit a boater in the head. Several had fallen into the water unconscious and been torn to shreds by their own propellers. Everyone was horrified by these fish. We asked if anyone ate them and the fishermen actually shuddered. "They're no good to eat—they're just blood and bones and weird ooze," said one of the guys. "If you get one in the boat they're hard to kill. They just jump around in the boat and bleed all over everything." The motors attracted them, the fishermen told us—the fish were driven crazy by the vibrations in the water if you motored where it was too shallow. That invisible line where the fish stopped was probably where the bottom dropped off, and it was deep enough to motor without vibrating the fish into insanity. The fishermen were sympathetic, and gave us bottles of Bud Light with Lime and a can of cocktail weenies.

I wished this experience had cured me of my fear of fish flying through the air. It did not. I can't say what would have happened if we had not had the cage on the boat and I had been hit with fish and had to pick up live fish as they flopped around the boat, bleeding and dying, and try to throw them in the water. I would be a different person than I am today if that had been the case. But, the cage protected us. I'm not sure about the moral of the story. I was worried all my life about the possibility of fish flying at me unexpectedly, then it happened. The only real change is that my fear of being forced to bite down on the tail of a live fish no longer seems so implausible. At some point, through some bizarre series of events, it's going to happen.

"WE ENCOUNTERED MANY OF WHAT I CALL 'MISSOURI MEN' FISHING WITH DYNAMITE." —Bella

WAVERLY. CAMPED AT MILE 293.5 NEXT TO THAT BOAT RAMP, THE "PORT OF WAVERLY RECREATION PARK."

A decent place for boaters, it has a nice park with picnic benches, fresh water spigot, power outlets, even a bathroom. Fancy. Waverly has a fruit market up the highway and an excellent view from atop the hill in town—look for the water tower! A library, a grocery, a pizza dumpster. Practically paradise. *The Two Headed Dog* had to fix a broken paddle here, a funny coincidence, because apparently those old colonial thugs Lewis and Clark had to fix a paddle here too.

CAMP AT MILE 285, BAKER'S BEND. A sweet beach! Fern and Bella harvested lots of wild grapes here and wild edible greens: goosefoot, stinging nettle and wood nettle. We harvested and ate a lot of these berries and greens. For identification of wild edible plants in the Mississippi River Basin, I recommend *FORAGER'S HARVEST* by Samuel Thayer. This is the best book about eating wild foods that I've read.

CAMP AT MILE 262, UPPER MIAMI BEND. Friendly townies at this camp spot. We walked across a bridge to the town of Miami on the south side of the river and found a Trading Post with a sweet breakfast deal and 50-cent ice cream.

"WE GOT A HUGE BOLT OF FABRIC, RED LEOPARD PRINT, THAT ENDED UP BEING A CANOPY, HOT PANTS AND MINI SKIRTS." —Bella

MILE 250. Totally awesome beach for swimming at the mouth of the Grand River. We spent a day here and built a minimal roof structure with willow sticks and rolled tarps over it. While on the move, we can roll up the tarps and clamp them to the roof boughs. We installed side panels for waterproofing from waves and rain. Lots of goosefoot growing here.

THE FIRST STORM. In the morning, we went two miles downriver, to Mile 248, Grand River Bend. Here, we saw a menacing cloud appear from behind, dark green and deep, so we headed for shore, quickly tied up the boat and set up tents. I had been watching the storm front move in and was looking at the river as it struck. I'd never seen anything like it. Terrifying. On the ocean they call it a "white squall"—a storm that seems to come from nowhere. As we stood in a dead calm, the storm front roared towards us through the trees on shore with a horrifying noise, and the mirror-like water rose instantly to become endless lines of two-foot waves ramming directly into our side. Thunder! Lightning! Chaos.

WE PULLED *THE SAUCER* OUT OF THE WATER TO STOP IT FROM BEING BATTERED AGAINST *The Snowball*. ALL SIX OF US HUNKERED DOWN INSIDE THE INSUBSTANTIAL ROOF OF *The Snowball*. The storm front snapped several main willow branches and the roof sagged down upon us. In the howling winds, we held on to the tarp roof of *The Snowball* to keep it from flying away! We drank year-old banana wine, which tasted good, and smoked what smokes we had. We were humbled. We had a storm party in the small space of the boat. These are always intimate affairs of mad laughter and excessive drunkenness. Trying to photograph it never conveys the essence of the experience—the camaraderie of having put oneself into an irrevocable situation of unknown peril.

The wind howled and the opposite shoreline disappeared in the grinding clouds, windblown waves battered the boat. Epic. After the storm calmed we went outside and found amusement in the shape of the roof, you could tell which way the wind was blowing by the direction the roof was leaning.

MILE 243, BUSHWACKER BEND. We saw *The Two Headed Dog* and stopped to chat. They had found two stray plastic decoy ducks which are now tied to their boat and are named "Stewart" and "Belinda."

THE ACCURSED ROCKET STOVE. ROCKET

STOVES FOCUS A SMALL AMOUNT OF BURNING WOOD TO COOK FOOD. A HANDFUL OF SMALL TWIGS ARE SUFFICIENT TO BOIL WATER. *I have cooked with sticks while camping in the past, but the setup was not efficient, with most of the heat spreading out in all directions.* The rocket stove focuses the heat straight up to the stovetop. Using rocket stoves for cooking, we planned to spend no money on cooking fuel; the energy of the sun, stored up in small twigs, would be all that was needed.

These rocket stoves were made using large and small tin cans. The inside of the stove has an L-shaped chimney, which is surrounded by sand to insulate and focus the heat upwards to the stove top. The cracks in the tin are stuffed with clay so the sand won't leak out. A flat piece of tin lying in the bottom of the fire hole allows air to circulate from under the sticks and burn the ends of the sticks. It keeps the fire from going out and is the source of the hot burning "rocket" effect.

The tools I used to make these were tin snips, a screwdriver and sheet metal screws, and pliers.

After taking these stoves down the Missouri River on our homemade pontoon boat, I have a good amount of experience with them. The type and size of wood you put in the stove makes all the difference. The first time I fired it at the Crooked Hat in Kansas City it blazed away, making a sound like a rocket! Then the whole time on the river it mostly just smoked a lot. We never saw dry wood once on the river and the damp wood kept smoking.

Drying the wood in the sun and keeping it in a sealed bucket to keep the moisture out of it is important. Splitting the wood with a small hatchet or sharp knife is important too, split wood burns much better than the outside of round sticks, which are more fire resistant than the inside grain of wood.

It took awhile for the rocket stove to heat up, but once all the sand insulating the stove heated up, the stove was easier to keep going. My favorite thing to start a rocket stove with: wax cardboard, such as fruit often comes in at the grocery store. I also tore a small tube off our abandoned umbrella and we used this to blow through—bellows for the fire. Never quite as hot as a constantly burning conventional stove, but there was ever-present moisture in the air, permeating the sticks we cooked with.

In two months, we never spent a dime on cooking fuel of any kind, and the wood burning rocket stove worked safely on an 8x20' boat with four people and a dog on it. I built a shroud around the stoves with flexible fresh willow boughs and some heavy canvas to direct the smoke away from the living space.

On shore we usually dug a small channel in the sand and put a grill over the top of that with a fire below, easier to stick random wood into it and hotter than the rocket stoves. Not as fuel efficient, but just the thing when you're in a hurry to get some food. The rocket stoves required some patience.

"PEAT WIRED UP A MINI CAST IRON SKILLET TO THE ENGINE AND FRIED AN EGG!" —Bella

MILE 226.5, GLASGOW. ONE HUNDRED AND THIRTY-SEVEN MILES DOWNRIVER FROM OUR LAUNCH POINT IN KANSAS CITY, I AM WRITING TO YOU FROM THE OLDEST LIBRARY WEST OF THE MISSISSIPPI. *Glasgow has it all, and it has it all within a six-block radius. A sweet river town with kind people, it seems like the towns that still have a connection to the river and aren't afraid of it are full of kind people.* Towns that retreat up to the hilltops and wall off the river, they seem disconnected; angry; hateful. How can you live near such a massive river and be afraid of it?

We fluffed up our provisions and are planning a roof raising party tonight to replace the roof blown off by the hellacious storm that shot lightning bolts down and swirled with that dark green tornado hue; that had winds thrashing the leaves of the trees like they had done something wrong.

Today, Peat and I took THE SAUCER to get more wood to brace up the new roof, and while on shore at a driftwood pile, Peat pointed out a snake. We got closer and it lunged at us! We jumped back, but noticed that the snake had something sticking out of its mouth—a pair of frog legs! The snake was perhaps only irritated about having its dinner hour disturbed. We laughed our asses off, like any rude dinner guest would.

"THINGS ARE GOING PRETTY GOOD, EXCEPT FOR THE MOSQUITOES AND HAVING TO CONSTANTLY TRAIN WILLARD, THE GIANT PUPPY. ANOTHER BEAUTIFUL DAY ON THE RIVER." —From the Log Book

MILE 217.5 SALINE CITY BEND. EIGHTY-FIVE DEGREES AND DRINKING BEER! We waited until the sun went down and when it was cool enough to work, we completely tore the busted roof off and replaced it with a sturdy one. In the morning, *The Snowball* was reborn! I started to wake up with the sun, and I'm not a morning person, so I took a picture of the rising sun. It looks just like the setting sun, in a photograph. A beaver swam back and forth, slapping its tail to alert the rest of the beavers that there were some strangers on the water.

MILE 205, SLAUGHTERHOUSE BEND. Not much of a beach. The water patrol shows up and checks our paperwork. Ya can't win 'em all!

"THE WATER PATROL WAS IMPRESSED THAT WE HAD A MINNESOTA BOAT LICENSE, AND SAID WE WERE 'BETTER THAN THE LAST BUNCH THEY'D SEEN.'" —Bella

MILE 186.5, ROCHEPORT BENDS. A sweet beach. Swimming on a sandy beach. We found wood nettle and stinging nettle in the bush; also some mosquitoes. Welcome to the water! There is a bike trail here that was formerly a railroad line, it goes nearly all the way from Kansas City to St. Louis.

"We had some flash flooding and all smashed up onto the boat to sleep. Our basil and pepper plants—that we put on shore to make room for sleeping—got carried away..." —Bella

MILE 170, PROVIDENCE BEND, COOPER'S LANDING. We arrived soggy and wet. Climbing the bank

we found some friendly locals at Cooper's Landing. They sold single beers, snacks, and Thai food. A bunch of party minded locals came down to *The Snowball* that evening and we had a smoking and drinking boat party. Tall tales were told. Ghost stories! Bigfoot? We covered life, the universe, and everything.

MILE 143.5 JEFFERSON CITY, THE CAPITAL OF MISSOURI. From the river we saw nothing but the tall round dome rising from a forest. We tied up just downriver from the highway bridge over the river. Everyone slogged through the mud to get to town. Fern and Bella went in circles in the mud and then came back to the boat, defeated. We all piled in *THE SAUCER* and canoed up Wears Creek, passing through an arch with train tracks over the top, and into the fabulous canals of Jefferson City. The canals were beautiful, dangling vines and wide beautiful arches. Completely neglected, I imagined that only a few of the citizens of this city had ever been down here.

We tied up *THE SAUCER* in the canal one block from the capital building, found an Italian buffet, and consumed mass quantities. I went back and grabbed the red five-gallon gas can. Looking up at that shining white dome of the capital and at the suits walking the streets around me, I expected at any moment a team of Homeland Security agents to swoop out and detain me, saying, "Why the hell are you walking around with a gas can?" I found the thought amusing, because even if that did happen, once I told the agents that I was "going down the river" they would hoot and shake my hand and say, "Damn! I always wanted to do that!"

Jefferson City was a big river city, no one looked strangely at us, and no one approached us with the small river town friendliness. In a city of this size, I was just some weirdo with a gas can. They see it every day.

"WE WERE BOATING IN THE RAIN AND ALMOST TO JEFFERSON CITY, A MILE OR SO AWAY AND THE WHOLE RIVER WAS FILLED WITH GIANT ROUND HAY BALES. I THOUGHT IT WAS SO COOL AND SURREAL. I HAD A DIFFICULT TIME GETTING INTO JEFF CITY. WE WALKED THROUGH THE SWAMP FOR A LONG TIME AND THEN HAD TO CROSS THE TRACKS. BUT WE HAD TO GET OUT OF THERE BECAUSE THAT CAMP SITE WAS SO SHITTY AND MUDDY AND IT HAD BEEN RAINING ALL DAY..." —Zoe

MILES 144-124. No entries in the log book because it was left out in the rain and had to dry for a few days. The log book is also the river chart book. We had to look at watercolor washed impressions of the river instead of precise and legible charts, because we printed the chart papers on a computer printer at the library instead of ordering the durable charts with waterproof ink from the Corps of Engineers. If you can afford it, I recommend professionally printed charts.

MILE 117, CHAMOIS BEND. A boat ramp with fresh water spigot, a swing set, and edible evening primrose flowers/buds.

Mile 97.5, Hermann Bend, Hermann.

We pulled into the mouth of Frene Creek, under the train bridge (Union Pacific coal trains, CSX, and Amtrak) at Mile 97.5, looking for a secluded camp spot. After climbing the muddy bank, we arrived in a nice grass-covered park, and said, "Hermann! Yes!" The most luxurious boat facility yet. Power outlets, bathroom open 24 hours, picnic pavilion, and grocery store (Save-A-Lot) one block from the river with food dumpster in back. There were coffee shops, "Time For Pie," or closer to the train bridge where we were camped was Sophie's. Hermann has a library, gas station, hardware store, and deli with ice cream. In the hot Missouri summer, we were always excited for ice cream. After being on the river for days, camping out, coming into a town was an amazing thing. The conveniences people took for granted we found to be precious. "Ah! A fresh water spigot! Now we can drink! What's that you say? ICE CREAM? Waahoo!"

We had such fun in town that we only got two miles downriver before camping at Mile 94.8.

"FERN AND I WENT ON A WINE TOUR WALKING IN OUR MUD-CAKED-UP-TO-OUR-KNEES-RIVER-RAT OUTFITS AND GOT RATHER TIPSY... THE WINERY HAD A LIMESTONE CELLAR AND OLD PEOPLE THAT THOUGHT FERN AND I HAD COME FROM MARS." —Bella

Mile 67.8 20 Days Out. We made it to Washington, Missouri today, home of a fine old library. *The Snowball* and *The Two Headed Dog* were safely tied up to the rocky bank. Immediately upon stumbling up to the top of the bank, a fellow in a car stopped to chat. He'd gone down the river and out on the ocean. He gave Peat a ride to the marina, looking for a prop to get our third engine running. The space shuttle has triple backup systems, and so would we. St. Louis was a wild bottleneck in the river right after the Missouri River joins it, so the extra thrust could put us into the proper orbit as we pass over the wreck of *The Circle Of Death*, an appropriately named shanty boat a friend of ours nearly went down with a couple of years ago.

Everything is better with Stag beer. If only we could have been sponsored by them, and then picked up a case or two in every town... maybe there is something to the big money boat trip thing. Aw, hell. I canoed into town and watched from the top of the bank as *The Snowball* came to shore. It was a terrifying sight! The current was sweeping it down, the 3.5 horse-power motor working for the shore! The boat—only eight feet wide by 20 feet long—looked so tiny on the big river, back in the driveway in Kansas City, it seemed huge, like we could each build our own cabin on the deck!

We built a new, sturdy roof that seemed waterproof; ready for the next raging fist of atmosphere to massage our blue tarps. The zipper on my tent blew out, jammed with mud and sand. I sewed up the zipper and cut out the screen from the door. I went in through the window after that. Peat sleeps on the boat under a mosquito net, because his tent was busted. Maybe Ged clawed a hole in it. Fern and Bella shared a tent. Zoe and Savannah alternated: one sleeping on the boat, one in a tent. After the storms, the river dropped—five feet one night. I awoke to see *The Two Headed Dog* with enough space to crawl underneath it. Savannah woke up wondering why her head was lower than her feet, then turned around and went back to sleep. It was a small aluminum boat and so it was easy to slide it off the shore. Our boat, with the plywood pontoons, was not so easy to slide. But everything was so muddy we just loosened the rope and oozed back into the river.

Been foraging a decent amount, goosefoot, stinging nettle, wood nettle, evening primrose, wild grapes. —Log Book

MILE 60. WE PASSED AN ISLAND WITH A CABIN ON IT.

A guy came out and got in his flat bottom boat and cruised out to meet us. He had a green camo shirt and mesh hat, 115hp engine. That thing could haul ass. He was curious to see what was going down the river.

MILE 48, PARADISE ISLAND.

A must-stop for every shanty boater! An island covered with nothing but sand and willow trees. A magical, tropical place. Set up and lovingly cared for by locals as a fishing and party location, there were skulls of giant catfish hanging from trees and set on top of stakes stuck in the ground. Willard and Ged were loving it. If you stop by here, please be respectful of Paradise Island. The evening we got here, we each took a hit of acid but it turned out to be bunk, thankfully! Acid is gross.

MILE 28, SAINT CHARLES.

We tied our boats to a shore covered in pieces of a glass-like substance, in times past there used to be a foundry at the top of the bank, and they dumped the slag down to the river. The Katy bike trail that started in KCMO runs right past this spot at the top of the bank.

We met some folks at a coffee shop downtown. We were invited back to their home—the Franklin House—full of local anarchist types, who were very friendly to us. They came and visited our boat and gave us lots of food and even some hot pepper plants to replace the ones we lost in the flood! They cooked an awesome breakfast and we got to take showers too. We love you, Franklin House people! Three cheers!

In the morning, one of them wanted to come with us on the boat for a couple days, and without asking the other crew what they thought I said, "Hop aboard!"

MILE 14.5, PELICAN BEND: THE TWO HEADED DOG GOES TO THE BOTTOM. OUR CAMPSITE

WAS AT THE HEAD OF PELICAN ISLAND, A BEAUTIFUL BEACH WITH GOOD CAMPING IN THE TREES. The idea of going into the Pelican Island Chute to camp turned out to be a bad one: the water had risen in the night and the current was too strong for us to get back upriver and out into the main channel! Down the Pelican Island Chute was a line of rocks that went from shore to shore: certain doom! *The Two Headed Dog* blazed up river and out to the main channel easily with their sleek little boat. *The Snowball* struggled with both engines blazing, all 8.5hp pushing five people and one big dog. Not happening. We decided to take it near the shallows at the head of the island and jump out, then pull the boat with ropes. Hella-old-school upriver-rafting technique. Terrifying as this was, we did it. I sounded the depth with an oar—about 3 feet. I grabbed a rope and jumped in, confident about what lay on the bottom because the previous evening I had taken a walk on the now submerged sandbar. It looked like I was jumping into the middle of the river and everyone looked at me in horror until they saw I was standing less than waist deep.

The fellow from St. Charles the night before, Dave, wanted to ride on *The Snowball* until St. Louis, but he wasn't expecting this! I have to commend him: Once he saw there was a bottom to walk on, Dave jumped in the water and pulled the boat along with Fern and Bella while Peat worked the motors and rudder.

Victory and total triumph! We climbed back on and *The Snowball* did a hard right turn as we hit the racing current of the main channel. The clouds parted and the sun shone down upon us. Yes! Smiles all around and everything seemed right in the universe.

Our celebration was short lived. Cruising onward we noticed two figures on the north bank yelling at us.

"What's up with those yahoos?!" I asked.

"What are they saying?" Peat wondered.

"Hey! Maybe they're trying to give us beers!" I said.

"That's Savannah and Zoe!" Peat said.

"What?"

I looked through the binoculars that Peat handed me and saw it was true: Zoe's dog Willard was there, too. Scanning further down the bank, a long line of white five-gallon buckets and other items from their boat floated down the river. A chill swept over my body.

The Two Headed Dog had sunk.

The present situation seemed to be the best outcome of a worst-case scenario. Their boat was nowhere in sight, it must have been at the bottom of the river. A catastrophe. And yet all hands were safely ashore!

We hauled into shore and picked them up. There was no need for immediate explanation. We shared the shock with them. "Are you alright? Do you need anything? Booze, yes of course, and cigarettes? Yes. Is Willard alright? Okay, good."

Peat took to *The Saucer* and paddled after the drifting buckets and managed to recover almost all of them.

After Zoe and Savannah had a moment to catch their breath we listened to their shocking story. While attempting to wait for us to join them, *The Two Headed Dog* threw anchor and the strong current on the outside of the bend sucked the anchor under and swamped their aluminum john boat within seconds. Zoe grabbed her dog, Willard, from the sinking vessel and they all swam to shore.

After Peat returned with the floating salvage, someone said, "Well, this isn't such a good campsite here. Who wants to go boating?"

We shoved off and motored down, riding low with all seven people and two big dogs aboard *The Snowball*. I saw a white bucket stuck in a pile of driftwood and took off in *The Saucer* after it. With the recovered bucket full of goodies in the canoe I paddled across the river. In the swift current it took a mile of river to get to the other side.

Landing at Sioux Passage Park at Mile 10.3, Dave, the guy we picked up in St. Charles, was able to offer a car ride into St. Louis from a relative. We received word that the river would rise eight feet. We looked down at the boat. Eight feet would be up to the level of the grass in the park. Any higher than that, and the entire park would be underwater. If we stayed here, we might have to climb into the trees.

We said our goodbyes to Zoe, Savannah, and Willard as they left with Dave and his dad to be dropped at the Bolozone in St. Louis. There, they could relax and make plans for what to do with the rest of their charmed lives.

The crew of *The Snowball* remained with the boat overnight. I slept the sleep of one who must not sleep, waking up every hour to look out the window of my tent at the top of the bank and the rising water. In the morning I found that the site I selected to pitch the tent was six inches above the river level! Holy fuck! The sight of the river climbing up to meet us was terrifying. We watched massive gluts of driftwood the length of a city block with old white refrigerators stuck in them floating down the flooded Missouri River.

At dawn, I stoked the coals of the campfire and made coffee. *As I finished the first cup, the rising water slid into the fire pit and extinguished the fire. It seemed like a good time to pack up and get out.*

Fern and Bella awoke in their tent surrounded by water several inches deep. The cry went out from inside the nylon walls, "*Oh noooooo!*" Good morning campers! Peat wisely slept on the boat. We packed up and talked on *The Snowball* as the water continued to take over the park. We watched single giant logs and whole piles, red nun buoys ripped from their cables, and a number of lonesome white refrigerators bobbing their way down to the Gulf. The road leaving the park would soon be flooded out and we faced the prospect of spending a week on the boat. We decided that it would be more fun to go hang out with Zoe and Savannah at the Bolozone—sanctuary for soggy sailors!

I scouted the road out of the park and then returned to *The Snowball* with bad news: it seemed like the chute could soon overflow the entire park with a river of rushing water. I suggested we pack faster. We loaded our gear into my canoe, *The Saucer*, and pulled it through knee high water that filled the park. The road to high ground was covered with what seemed to be gently flowing water from the large chute behind Pelican Island. We crossed the flooded road two at a time in *The Saucer*. Looking down that flooded road filling with river water and thinking about wading to the other side, I thought, "This is how people die." I was glad we had the canoe. You look and think, "Oh, it's shallow and mellow," only to find a wild undercurrent in the middle that sweeps you away. We were fortunate that the current was flowing towards high ground. We made it to the steps into the park and chained *The Saucer* to a tree, then climbed into a field of green grass and sunshine. We laid out our wet clothes to dry and had time to contemplate.

I have never been so happy to get off the river.

Some jerks working in the park insulted us for not knowing the river was dangerously flooding and called the park rangers on us, who stopped us in squad cars as we left the park on foot. The rangers, upon hearing our story, apologized for running our ID's and commended us for attempting the journey! We bid them good day and continued on our rush-hour bike trek into the heart of the beast. Peat had to walk with his old dog Ged. When we arrived at the Bolozone we found Peat drinking a beer, hanging out with Zoe and Savannah! Turns out Peat hitched a ride with a Lewis and Clark re-enactor who had a dug-out canoe on top of his truck and demonstrated the flint and steel technique of starting a fire while he was driving! As the ball of frayed hemp twine caught fire, he tossed it out the window. Strange world. The man was happy to have rescued a fellow river rat and took Peat directly to his destination. We got a large case of our favorite beer, Stag, and built a fire at the Bolozone, our sanctuary in St. Louis. We hung out with our old and new friends, happy around the campfire, just like every night for the last month on the river.

Ged and Willard were happy to see each other.

WASHED-UP IN ST. LOUIS. *THE SNOWBALL*

SPENT A WEEK ON ITS OWN, TIED TO A PAIR OF LARGE COTTONWOOD TREES AT THE TOP OF THE BANK, RIDING OUT THE HIGH WATER. *When the water goes below flood stage, we will return and figure out what to do with our boat.*

I rode my bike down to the waterfront and walked the steps below the famous stainless steel arch. The water had climbed up the steps and covered the road, then climbed the steps again. The flood was at its crest and the road below, usually illuminated by streetlights, had its power shut off and was sealed off by concrete flood walls and the metal flood doors which had been closed and sealed to prevent the old town part of St. Louis from flooding. The U.S. and State of Missouri flags flew from flag poles that were almost halfway underwater. The tops of street signs protruded from the water, "No Parking Zone." Out in the wide flooded river huge logs and driftwood piles and strange pieces of debris floated down. The river was closed, you could only go out on it if your boat had 3500hp, meaning only towboats performing some kind of emergency work.

I was walking inside the floodwall, finding the closed floodgates heavily sand bagged and slightly leaking. I climbed the metal struts to the top of the gates and looked down at the river. I thought about our escape from the river the previous day, our 8x20' plywood shanty boat our only haven from this massive downward flow of water. There wasn't a single person in the city who wouldn't think we were mad. We didn't have access to communication on *The Snowball*, no weather radios, internet phones, etc. It was obvious that the water was rising, but we didn't know it was going to serious flood stage until we landed in Pelican Park and Dave's dad told us. We weren't trying to be hardcore or anything. It's just that weather radios and batteries cost money. We were in it for the long haul and wanted to conserve! After our experience on *The Snowball*, I would recommend that everyone have a fully functioning weather radio with extra batteries as essential gear, right after life jackets. What the weather radio will tell you is what the weather is like upstream from where you are, which is what is important for flooding! You could be on the river, dry as a bone, and end up in a catastrophic flood if it's been dumping down upriver from you!

It's good to do different things, keeps your mind working, synapses firing.

I was on a break from the river now, waiting for all the water dumped upstream in the great Mississippi Basin to make its way down to the Gulf—and it was taking its time. The crew of *The Two Headed Dog* called it quits and went back to Minneapolis to work and play, dragging along Peat, Fern, and Bella, too. I was in St. Louis with *The Snowball,* but I had no plans to go visit the boat. It was either gonna be there or be gone when we all met back there in a week. It's bad luck to go peeking on it now.

I was loving St. Louis; hanging out with people; exploring the city; sitting in Black Bear Bakery drinking coffee and writing this novel I've been working on all winter, spring, and summer. Somebody remind me never to write an 800 page novel again, please.

I fixed a garden hose today for the house next door called The Momo. I stepped on the damn thing the first night here and water went gushing everywhere! Hard times with water lately. After two attempts, I got it working, still a little drip coming out. It was sad having everyone gone, but good after being on a boat the size of a small bedroom with four other people and a large dog for a month.

"I learned to be happy alone. Sometimes that means I don't know how to be happy around other people, so I just want to be with myself, because it's easier that way, not having to deal with anyone. I have learned to talk to myself very well. I am a good listener." —Log Book

HOW LONG HAVE I BEEN IN ST. LOUIS? DAMN, A WEEK NOW. *Continuing on with my summer writing adventure, the novel continues and the story follows where I am in reality.* The characters are in St. Louis, their boat tied up on the river. *Ha! It's a fun way to write, and feels more real than following an outline which would force the story to go in a predetermined direction. I can do anything with this story now that I'm in it.*

Holed up in the "Boat Kid's Suite" at the Bolozone, a large room at the rear where the electronic musical instrument pedal shop used to be, I whacked on the typewriter. Sometimes Alyssa or Billy would come and find me, and made me eat food. Sometimes the fastest cat ever, Cookies, visited me. Lots of varmints last night, the dog across the alley kept barking at something rummaging around. Raccoon? Possum? Sleeping on this futon on the floor, I woke up as something ran across my neck, leaving burning claw marks. Fucking rodent! Rat! Tiny demon! Cookies, where were you when I needed you? Why would a mouse do that—some kind of a dare? Maybe it was Cookies who ran across my neck.

The crew of *The Snowball* came back the next day. Good. I started to think about getting a job and settling down there. It wouldn't be so bad.

"MANY THANKS TO DAN, ALYSSA, BILLY, AND EVERYONE ELSE IN ST. LOUIS FOR HELPING US OUT. THANKS TO THE BOLOZONE AND THE MOMO, WHOSE DOORS ARE ALWAYS OPEN FOR RIVER REFUGEES TO FLOAT IN." —Log Book

"WHEN WE RETURNED FROM MINNEAPOLIS AFTER THE FLOOD WE DUMPSTERED A BUNCH OF FERMENTING PINEAPPLES AND STARTED A BUCKET OF HOOCH..." —Bella

The Snowball **Rolls On!** Return to The Snowball. Was it still there? I had been wondering all week if our journey was over. My intuition told

me the boat was fine. We tied it up in a good place, sturdy old cottonwoods. We knew how high the river would crest. Unless those cottonwoods fell over, *The Snowball* would be fine. When we returned and drove out to Sioux Passage Park we ran into the same park ranger that commended us a week ago as we evacuated. We found the formerly flooded parking lot and road were now covered with river mud. A set of tractor tire tracks cut through the goop for us to walk out there. The cool thing about the ground being covered in mud is you can see all the tracks of the animals that walked there: deer tracks everywhere, birds, mice, raccoon, beavers, coyotes, dogs, and some I didn't recognize. Our canoe was safely stashed in the trees, but now we had to portage it all the way back to the river. Oh dammcit! A 16' long fiberglass canoe is heavy! I talked to a couple park workers in a truck, unlike the first two on the day of evacuation who called the rangers on us, these guys were friendly and curious.

The Snowball was still there, balanced precariously on the edge of a muddy shelf! The rear ends of the pontoons stuck a few feet over open air! Two large cottonwood trees and ropes held *The Snowball* while the water went down, bringing the boat to a perfectly balanced resting spot, like something out of a Charlie Chaplin movie. We could walk around on deck and it would move around, like it was still on the water, but it wouldn't actually fall either way.

Great, we still had a boat, and nobody looted it! *Now, how did we move the boat down 50 feet of slope to get it back into the Missouri River? Roll it!*

Peat had gone to return the rental car, so Fern, Bella, and I began collecting round logs and sticks to make a "Corduroy Highway" to roll *The Snowball* on. First, we laid down a surface of sticks and branches and long little logs into the mud to be the roadway, then fatter rounds jammed up under the pontoons to be the wheels. Some people think this is how the Egyptian pyramids were built.

Everything was ready. Bella and Fern were skeptical. I convinced them to give it a shove and we were all a little shocked as *The Snowball* began heading down the bank, making it halfway before grinding to a dead halt.

"Break time!"

After some climbing around underneath the boat, between the pontoons, I found a chunk of driftwood sticking up from the mud, holding the starboard pontoons. This was a good thing since it saved half of the boat-rolling for Peat. When he returned from town we pried from the side and off it went! Victory! *The Snowball* hit the water and its ass was floating, then with the final shoves we heard a terrible splitting noise as the starboard pontoon cracked in half! Possibly damaged from that driftwood encounter on the hill. Good thing the pontoons were full of foam. The next day we squeezed it back together and screwed it shut with a plywood patch.

We were all very happy that night, celebrating the second launching of THE SNOWBALL. Every day since Savannah, Zoe, and Willard left has been strange and lacking though. We toasted to our departed comrades and *The Two Headed Dog*. Half of the flotilla was gone. It wasn't even a "flotilla" anymore, just a "float." Sigh. We miss you.

BEFORE.   AFTER.

I SLEEP WITH THE SUN. *I GO TO SLEEP SHORTLY AFTER DARK AND WAKE WITH THE SUNRISE NOW. WHEN THE SUN SLEEPS, SO DO I. THAT'S OLD SCHOOL. LIVING OUTSIDE, WITHOUT ELECTRICITY, CLOSE TO THE NATURAL CYCLES OF THE PLANET AS IT SPINS. INTERESTING. I HAVE NEVER SEEN SO MANY SUNRISES. USUALLY WHEN I SEE THE SUN RISE, IT'S BECAUSE I HAVE STAYED UP ALL NIGHT!*

Today we floated down to join with the Mississippi River, make a right turn, and head south. We all felt sadness, *The Two Headed Dog* should have been here. Before passing through downtown St. Louis we passed through the one and only Lock and Dam #27, the last one on the upper river. All free flow from here on down.

"I FIND GREAT BLUE HERON MUDDY FOOT ART ON THE BLEACHED WHITE WOOD OF A FALLEN-OVER COTTONWOOD TREE THAT RESTS HERE ATOP THE BEACH WHERE HIGH WATER LEFT IT. THIS GREAT BLUE HERON ART PIECE WAS DONE DURING THE NIGHT, I AWOKE TO FIND IT IN THE MORNING, THREE TOES DIPPED IN MISSISSIPPI MUD, CAREFULLY STAMPED ONTO THE WOOD OF THAT OLD TREE. WHAT WAS THE BIRD TRYING TO CONVEY WITH THIS PIECE? WHO AMONG US CAN UNDERSTAND A BIRD BRAIN? COULD THE HERON POSSIBLY HAVE STEPPED IN THE MUD AND THEN ONTO THE EMPTY CANVAS OF THAT LOG WITH NO CONSCIOUSNESS ABOUT THE PRINTS IT WAS MAKING? WE CAN MAKE ASSUMPTIONS, BUT WE CAN NEVER KNOW."
—Log Book

PASSING THROUGH THE DEADLY BOTTLENECK OF ST. LOUIS. *Every shanty boater has a similar terrifying experience passing through St. Louis. The river narrows through the city and the current increases, the shores lined with wall-to-wall square steel barges and the towboats are bustling back and forth, churning up the water with thousands of horse power.* It's like a river full of 20,000 horses doing the dogpaddle, that each shanty boater must navigate. The wakes of the towboats are not so terrible on the open river, but with half a dozen towboats all contributing, without a shore for the waves to crash upon and expend their energy, the waves bounce off the steel sides of the moored barges and come back into the river amplified!

The Snowball encountered such a perfect wave storm south of the arch, waves over five feet ran at us as a big towboat pushed its load upstream, amplifying the waves buffeting us. The bow of *The Snowball* rose and fell as though we were on open ocean, water splashed over the bow and through the cabin. When the bow dipped down into a trough we could see nothing between the deck and the roof but a wall of water. From the rear of the boat, his hand on the tiller, Peat began to shout, "Oh god! I don't know! I don't know!"

I let off a rebel yell to boost morale, but I was scared too. *The Snowball* was being tested. "We got it, Peat! Keep it in the waves! Don't let us go sideways!"

"I think the engine is gonna be swamped!" Peat yelled back.

I had been looking straight forward the whole time. Now I looked to the aft as the bow rose on a wave and was shocked to see the rear of the boat dipping under water, inches from the engine!

"Oh fuck!" Without the engine to propel us, we would have little ability to steer, and the waves would push us sideways, and then *The Snowball* could be flipped over by a wave. If the boat were to flip, it wouldn't sink because the pontoons were full of foam and buckets, but that would definitely put us on the wrong side of things! Going for a swim amid the wild, swirling and sucking currents created by these machines was not appealing. I went to the front of the boat and held on, trying to allow the back of the boat more buoyancy. Fern and Bella moved closer to the front also and darted out to grab random items that broke loose from the boat and tried not to head overboard with each violent rocking of the boat. I watched the waves coming at us and listened for sound of our pontoons cracking in half.

I'm certain I wasn't the only one thinking about a friend of ours whose shanty boat was sunk at this very place by the surging waves created by towboats that came too close. That boat was top heavy, but ours was bottom heavy. We designed *The Snowball* to be unsinkable. Had we succeeded?

How long did that battle with the waves of the towboats go on? Five minutes? Ten minutes? When at last we motored beyond the waves and into relatively calm water, it felt like we had experienced an eternal moment of peril. To various degrees, we were all traumatized.

"DURING THE MAYHEM OF THE WAVES CRASHING OVER THE SIDE OF THE SNOWBALL, FERN AND I WERE HAND-DRILLING HOLES IN THE DECK (BETWEEN THE PONTOONS) TO DRAIN WATER. WE LOOKED OUT AT THE PELICANS SWIMMING ALONGSIDE THE BARGES, THEY WERE FLOATING JUST FINE WHILE WE WERE BEING FLOWN OUT OF THE WATER!" —
Bella

SOMEWHERE ON THE MISSISSIPPI. *We headed to shore one afternoon as a storm front rolled in, wild winds.* In the midst of the howling sky I stopped and looked up and saw a rapidly rotating spiral in the clouds directly above our camp. I laughed. There was nothing to be done. Water runs downhill, so the river was the lowest place, therefore the safest place to be in a tornado.

"WE ALL GOT INTO OUR TENTS AND TRIED TO STAY DRY. WE WERE PASSED OVER AND ARE STILL ALIVE TODAY. IF THERE WERE EXTERNAL FORCES AT WORK PROTECTING US OF WHICH I AM NOT AWARE, SUCH AS GUARDIAN ANGELS, I WOULD LIKE TO TAKE THIS MOMENT TO THANK THEM. OH YEAH, AND THANKS FOR THAT TWO HEADED DOG THING TOO." —Log Book

"I CONTEMPLATED TYING MYSELF TO A LARGE TREE IN FEAR OF BEING BLOWN AWAY. INSTEAD, I FILLED MY TENT WITH LOGS AND ZIPPED IT UP TIGHT. I STILL FEEL LUCKY TO BE ALIVE AFTER THAT DAY." —Peat

THE FOG AND THE MUD. *The night before the fog. Somewhere downriver from St. Genevieve in the boonies.* Only ours, blue heron, and coyote tracks on the beach.

In the morning through the fog the sound of engines idling, we heard the hum of towboats that took themselves to shore to wait out the impenetrable fog. As the sun burns the fog off we heard them rev up and return to the channel, free from the fog's grip.

The muddy bank welcomed us to Cape Girardeau. My foot went in up to the knee. The paper lantern pepper plant that Angela and Michael gave us in St. Charles was still kicking out peppers; it was a tiny sign of hope in this foggy muddy world we had entered.

"Tucked away up a drainage, nestled under the train bridge, we watch the towboats go by and their wake sends nothing more than a gentle ripple our way. A good spot, though the flooding has made a mud cake bake of the bank. The coffee in town at Grace Cafe is the finest. I was sad to go there and hear that they were closing down. Why do all the good things go away?" —Log Book

DAVEY AND PEAT.

"FERN AND I DUMPSTERED MAGAZINES WITH ALL KINDS OF RECIPES AND WOULD READ THEM TO EACH OTHER FOR BED TIME... IT MADE US HUNGRY FOR TREATS, SO WHEN WE GOT INTO TOWN WE WOULD GO CRAZY BUYING LITTLE DEBBIES AND CHOCOLATE... IF THE CHOCOLATE MELTED WE WOULD SNEAKILY SUCK UP THE CHOCOLATE IN OUR TENTS." — Bella. And everyone else would giggle wildly. Outside the tent, Peat and I would look at each other and shrug.

CAIRO! THE SOUTHERNMOST TOWN IN ILLINOIS. *There's always triumph in reaching the confluence of the Mississippi and Ohio rivers: Cairo.* I was here three years ago on *The Leona Joyce* with Paula and Caleb. It took us three months to get here back then. Now, starting from Kansas City, it had taken us a month and a week, with a week holed up in St. Louis waiting for the flood waters to go down so, really, just a month on the water, a new boat punk record probably.

Cairo is an interesting town of massive old marble and sandstone buildings alongside the totally decrepit ruins of a once wealthy downtown. Brick storefronts simply collapsed outwards onto the sidewalk and were left there to harbor weeds. Entire blocks of downtown were abandoned.

The public library was beautiful and staffed by the kind and wise librarians. Before the journey began, Bella had screened t-shirts for the crew that said, "Shantyboat University 2008." At the Cairo library the librarian asked if I was their professor, ha ha! I guess by then I had a good salt-n-pepper beard going. Those university shirts looked real; we could have gotten student discounts. Except for me, the "professor."

Also in Cairo is a massive three-story marble museum full of everything. The characters on the street are wild and conversational. Trees growing out of windows and doors of abandoned buildings, no money to even buy plywood to board them up, just rotten wood, broken glass, total decay. Cairo has an intense history. Being the confluence of two great rivers, Native Americans must have considered this a sacred place. White settlers created a capitalist boomtown during the steamboat days, then the railroads took that economy away. Violent racial riots occurred during the civil rights era, sparked by the framing of a black man for the death of a white girl. The black man died while in police custody, police claimed he killed himself. Much of the affluent white population left town. The exit of rich white people from Cairo left the town economically slumped and with a lingering anger over the continuing racial/class disparity.

MILE 934, WOLF ISLAND. WE MADE CAMP ON

Wolf Island, our first camp on the Lower Mississippi! Pretty excited to be somewhere we had never been before. None of us in our boating adventures before had ever been this far down. The combined Upper Mississippi and Ohio Rivers made for a wide beast of a river, with huge dikes of rock jutting out into the river on the inside of the bends. Attempts have been made by the Army Corps of Engineers to control the flow and siltation of the river, in order to maintain a deep enough shipping channel for the barges.

In the morning on Wolf Island, we met the owner of a small cabin that we saw up on higher ground. He was friendly. He told us that he owned the island, all 1400 acres of it, lived on 400 acres and rented out the other 1000. He said there were motion-activated cameras on his cabin so that if anyone tried to break in he would have pictures of what they looked like. He worked for the Corps of Engineers, and his cabin was attached with cables to the island so that when high floodwaters came and submerged the island, his cabin would simply float up and then back down. He could even come visit his cabin during a flood! He told us a story about trying to haul a 4-wheeled ATV on his john boat to the island but he swamped the boat and lost everything. Because he worked for the Corps, he had a buddy on a Corps towboat come up and they used a dredge crane to pull his ATV and boat off the bottom of the river! It must be nice. But then, maybe he can't take off three months to go down the river like we could? Being the seasonal/temp jobbers that we are. His cabin and land got us thinking though. He must have got the land hella cheap, because who would want to buy land that became covered in water at some time every year? We could get a hold of some undesirable land like that, and build floating cabins, yeah!

MILE 910, DAVEY! WE NOTICED A RED KAYAK

and a fellow on shore. *Five miles later we camped on a sandbar built up on a dike at Mile 904.5.* The guy in the red kayak showed up, and was named Davey. Originally from Scotland, Davey now lived in New York. He was going as far down the Mississippi River as he could, just as we were. He hung out, rode on *The Snowball* with us, and we drank lots of beers together. He bought us sandwiches too; a very kind fella. The previous year on his kayak adventure, Davey had found a dead body floating in the river and told the authorities about it. Hella creepy!

MILE 889, NEW MADRID. WHAT A STRANGE

TOWN. *We climbed up from the river and found* deserted *streets except for a middle-aged guy with a huge afro on a BMX bike, drinking beer from a can with a straw, slowly cruising around.* He was very kind. Being from the big city, I was suspicious. He only wanted to help though, he rode along with us and showed us the location of the Quick Sack store. The streets of downtown were eerily deserted. There were dried stalks of corn tied in large bunches to the telephone poles and light posts downtown. The wind rattled the dry cornhusks. The wind blew an old metal sign back and forth. Squeak. Squeak. Squeak. In this most vacant and creepy town the few people we did meet were overflowing with kindness; the man on the bike offered to bring us some blankets later that night if we needed any. The workers in the Quick Sack were good to us too.

Redneck Clothes Line. Cairo, IL

MILE 872, TIPTONVILLE. CAMPED WITH OUR NEW FLOTILLA PARTNER DAVEY AND HIS RED KAYAK AT THE RAMP. Davey headed into town to find the pub. Davey loved his pubs. In Scotland, he said, all business and social affairs are conducted in the pubs; that's just where you went to meet people and do things. It wasn't just a place to get wasted and party. It was business! And also you could drink a pint or two, which made life that much more fun.

"ONE OF DAVEY'S PUB-MATES CAME DOWN AND BROUGHT US BEER, THOUGH SHE HERSELF DIDN'T DRINK. SHE HAD JUST FINISHED ROOFING A BARN. A COOL WOODS LADY THAT RAISED WOLVES! FERN AND BELLA LOVED HER, SHE WAS A BAD-ASS." —Peat

MILE 845, CARUTHERSVILLE: THE SNOWBALL MELTS. *End of the line. Tired and broke. Caruthersville, Missouri.* We landed *The Snowball* on the downstream side of a massive wing dam and there, began to tear it down and prepare for leaving. Davey headed into town to find the pub and ask around if anybody wanted our pontoon boat. He got lost in the woods trying to get to the pub one night, ended up in what locals thought was a bad part of town, and he called his new friend from the pub. She said, "Stay RIGHT where you are, we are coming to pick you up!" Davey thought it was funny, being from New York.

Leaving our life on the river was strange. After 3 months you start to feel like a place is your home, even if it keeps floating downstream. Our home had become that raft, bouncing down the river, bordered by the banks on either side. That was our front and back yard, constantly changing but very reliable and the same every day. The thought of leaving that to go dwell in a city in some dingy house with a dingy job was repulsive but also fascinating. A house with hot and cold plumbing? Electricity? A roof? More than 3 other people to talk to? Wow. Caruthersville was an arbitrary end. We considered ending in Memphis, but after a conversation we decided it was time. Out of money and getting skinny from the meager food supply, we found a place in Caruthersville that would rent us a car to drive our stuff to Little Rock, Arkansas, where we could stay at a friend's house and make money working for a good old guy named Larry. After Savannah and Zoe left it wasn't as much fun. We kept going, just the four of us on that little raft, *The Snowball*. Three months, minus the time during the flood that we were in town. That was an achievement itself, and the four of us are still friends!

Eventually, Davey found us a fisherman at the pub who wanted to take *The Snowball* off our hands. Our idea of setting fire to it after taking the foam out to avoid leaving a piece of floating trash on the river was a bummer, we liked this outcome better. *The Snowball* would make a great fishing platform: or rock stage, party boat, barbecue pontoon, floating hunting blind, yoga and meditation surface, or perhaps all of these simultaneously. Long live *The Snowball* in its new home!

AFTER WE STRIPPED *THE SNOWBALL* DOWN TO THE PLYWOOD DECK AND OUR POSSESSIONS LAY SCATTERED ALL OVER THE DIKE, a coast guard buoy-tender ship passing by

noticed us, and seeing this mess of our possessions strewn on the beach, a piece of conversation was overheard coming from a sailor on the deck of their vessel, "Do they need help?" I laughed good at that one. It DID look like a shipwreck!

We decided to take a drive to Little Rock, Arkansas, dump our stuff in someone's backyard and visit old friends. Peat rented us a car, for which I was grateful. If there's one thing that's hard after a three month shanty boat journey, it's hitting the road with your thumb out.

Thanks to everyone who helped us out in Kansas City, The Crooked Hat, the house across the street, Jimmy who we met at Cooper's Landing and all the Cooper's Landing late-night drinkers, all the St. Charles anarchist people, the Bolozone in St. Louis, those random donations of food from river rats loitering around boat ramps, Davey from New York by way of Scotland. The photos were taken using a camera that Paula gave me. Thanks!

Essential Shanty Boat Advice

1) Here's the best advice we learned on the Missouri River: Where the current is strong, do not throw your anchor, it will drag your boat down. If you want to use your anchor, use it only on the INSIDE of the bend, where the current is milder. We used our anchor mainly to stick into the sand of beaches where there was no tree or rock to tie down to.

2) Try to camp on the inside of the bends, where the current is milder. The inside of the bend has beaches, since the strong current on the outside of the bend washes the sand downstream and deposits it on the inside of the next bend. It is also much more fun to swim on the inside of the bend, where you can relax and not be swept away.

3) If you are boating at night, have the proper lighting. Bigger and faster moving boats will destroy you. You might not plan to go boating at night, but if you get caught boating along looking for a good campsite at sunset, you might find yourself in darkness.

4) Have a life jacket for every person. If someone becomes stumbling drunk, they must wear the life jacket.

5) Drinking while boating is fun, like drinking and driving and drinking and train riding, but is also a frequent cause of death: your death, the death of ones you love, and the death of strangers. It's very easy to drown, people do it every day.

6) Have two methods of reliable propulsion. If one system fails, you have the backup. Do not be a one-legged person in an ass-kicking contest.

7) Plan for one gallon of water per person, per day. A food-grade five-gallon bucket with a lid works great.

Glossary

Wing Dam or Dike—On the Upper Mississippi people call them wing dams, on the Missouri and Lower Mississippi people call them dikes. I think it's a cultural thing, because there's not any difference. A wing dam or dike is a long line of wooden pilings or boulders that juts out into the river. The Army Corps of Engineers builds wing dams to control the flow of the river.

Main Channel—The deepest part of the river with the most rapid current, the result of engineering by the Army Corps of Engineers in order to create a reliable course for commercial shipping. Usually avoided by the shanty boater in favor of back channels where the horrors of modern civilization are less prevalent.

BELLA MOVED TO SEATTLE, LAUNCHED A FABULOUS CAREER IN FINE ARTS. SHE GOT A JOB AS A BOUNCER AT A GAY BAR.

FERN WAS LAST SEEN RIDING HER BIKE TOWARDS THE GULF OF MEXICO.

PEAT GOT A JOB IN LITTLE ROCK MOVING STUFF AROUND.

I GOT THE SAME JOB.

WILLARD BECAME A PHILOSOPHER.

ZOE AND SAVANNAH WENT MAD.